MILITARY JOBS

AIR FORCE COMBAT CONTROLLERS

What It Takes to Join the Elite

ALEXANDER STILWELL

Cavendish
Square
New York

Published in 2015 by Cavendish Square Publishing, LLC
243 5th Avenue, Suite 136, New York, NY 10016

© 2015 Brown Bear Books Ltd

First edition

Website: cavendishsq.com

This publication represents the opinions and views of the author based on his or her personal experiences, knowledge, and research. The information in this book serves as a general guide only. The author and publisher have used their best efforts in preparing this book and disclaim liability rising directly or indirectly from the use and application of this book.

CPSIA compliance information: Batch #WW15CSQ.

All websites were available and accurate when this book was sent to press.

Library of Congress Cataloging-in-Publication Data

Stilwell, Alexander.
 Air Force combat controllers : what it takes to join the elite / Alexander Stilwell.
    pages cm. — (Military jobs)
 Includes index.
 ISBN 978-1-50260-230-5 (hardcover) ISBN 978-1-50260-233-6 (ebook)
 1. United States. Air Force—Commando troops. 2. Close air support—Study and teaching—United States. 3. Special forces (Military science)—United States. I. Title.

 UG633.S785 2014
 358.4—dc23

                        2014026752

For Brown Bear Books Ltd:
Editorial Director: Lindsey Lowe
Managing Editor: Tim Cooke
Children's Publisher: Anne O'Daly
Design Manager: Keith Davis
Designer: Lynne Lennon
Picture Manager: Sophie Mortimer

Picture Credits:
T=Top, C=Center, B=Bottom, L=Left, R=Right

Front Cover : FC All images Library of Congress
All images © Library of Congress, except; 10, © Bettmann/Corbis; 30, © Shutterstock.

Manufactured in the United States of America

CONTENTS

INTRODUCTION

Combat Controllers are the Air Force's special forces. They work with other U.S. special forces deep inside combat zones and prepare the way for air assaults or direct air operations from the ground.

Combat Controllers have many roles. They establish assault zones where aircraft or parachutists can land, using controlled demolition to remove obstacles. They control communications with U.S. aircraft, identifying targets and calling in air strikes. They are qualified air traffic controllers, so they can direct aircraft movements even in a busy assault zone.

Combat Controllers often operate deep inside hostile territory and learn various ways to get into position. They are trained to live rough and travel light, using transportation such as motorbikes and all-terrain vehicles (ATVs). Combat Controllers enter the operational area with whatever special forces unit has been tasked with a particular mission. That means they have to be experts in the tactics and techniques used by all the other U.S. special forces.

 A Combat Controller uses camouflage to avoid detection in a an area of grassy scrubland.

HISTORY

Air Force Combat Controllers were originally "Pathfinders" in World War II (1939–1945). These expert teams prepared the way for parachute jumps into enemy territory.

 A group of Pathfinders study their map after landing by glider in Normandy during the D-Day landings in 1944.

Pathfinders marked a target area with beacons and flares, and reported on local weather conditions. They played a vital role in the D-Day invasion of Normandy on June 6, 1944. They were also involved in Operation Market Garden,

where U.S., British, and Polish forces attempted to capture the bridges over the Rhine into Germany. In the Pacific war, Pathfinders landed in gliders in the Burma jungle to create landing strips for long-range forces.

Korea and Vietnam

A Pathfinder Squadron was created during the Korean War (1950–1953). They helped get U.S. forces into and out of Korea. Combat Controllers also operated in the Vietnam War (1963–1975). They worked behind enemy lines, providing targeting information

 Combat Controllers keep lookout as they coordinate an air drop.

for aerial attacks on the Ho Chi Minh trail. This jungle route was used by the North Vietnamese to smuggle weapons to the South.

IN ACTION

Combat Controllers played a vital role in twenty-first-century conflicts in Afghanistan and Iraq. Many combat controllers won medals for gallantry—a reminder not only of their great skills but also of the dangers of their job.

▶▶ WHAT IT TAKES

When a Combat Controller is in a combat environment, he needs to remain calm enough to guide air operations under fire.

A combat controller's most powerful weapon is his radio. It links him to aircraft pilots who control devastating firepower. To make sure he can keep in touch with the air at all times, a Combat Controller has to be familiar with not only sophisticated communications equipment, but also digital networks and the latest targeting and surveillance equipment.

Avoiding the Enemy

A Combat Controller has one of the most dangerous jobs in the armed services. They often have to call in air strikes close to their own positions. Because they operate deep inside hostile territory, they also risk coming into direct contact with the enemy. They are trained to use a wide variety of weapons to

A Combat Controller rides in a helicopter on a mission in Afghanistan in 2003.

A Combat Controller studies the wind direction ahead of a parachute jump.

defend themselves. They are also trained in the stealth and evasion techniques they need to get into the combat zone.

Adaptability

Because Combat Controllers usually work alongside other special forces, they need to be adaptable. Different units have preferences for how to get into the combat zone, and the Combat Controller has to fit in with his colleagues. He also has to be able to liaise successfully with personnel from other units, or with local friendly forces in enemy territory. There are no women Combat Controllers, although this may change as the U.S. government reviews the role of women in the military.

EYEWITNESS

"In a nutshell, we're all battlefield airmen. If the fight on the ground's got anything to do with planes or helicopters, which they all do these days, we're there to coordinate it."

—Combat Controller, Iraq

▷▷ SPECIAL TACTICS SQUADRONS

Combat Controllers work with other U.S. Air Force special forces. They are trained to get into combat zones in any way—and to fight when they get there.

Combat Controllers belong to Air Force Special Tactics Squadrons (STS), which include specialists in three more roles vital for successful air assaults.

Pararescue

A pararescueman is a qualified paramedic. The U.S. Air Force boasts that their rescuemen are trained to find and save injured personnel "in any environment on the planet." Pararescuemen are also expected to be able to fight off the enemy while they care for and evacuate a patient.

▷▷ **Special Operations Weather airmen measure wind speed and direction.**

EYEWITNESS

"I was put on this earth to go out there and save that one person that no one else on this world could save and bring him home."

—**First Lieutenant Jeff, Combat Rescue Officer**

Special Operations Weather

These meteorologists are trained to carry lightweight weather equipment into the assault zone and use it in order to provide highly accurate reports on changing weather conditions deep behind enemy lines. These reports have to be reliable—the success or failure of an operation may depend on knowing how the weather is likely to change.

Tactical Air Control Party

These Controllers plan and control combat air resources for a ground mission. They advise the U.S. Army and other branches of the military on how the Air Force can help in a particular situation.

 A Combat Controller coordinates the movement of airplanes on a runway during an exercise.

>> COMBAT CONTROL SELECTION COURSE

U.S. Air Force Combat Controllers have a simple message, "Never quit." It is written on the walls of their gym and is shouted by instructors during punishing physical training.

The Combat Control Selection Course is designed to be tough. The Air Force only wants candidates who have the discipline to keep going when their minds and bodies are screaming at them to stop.

All candidates must have already fully completed the Air Force basic military training course. Despite that, at least 60 percent of candidates will quit during the ten-day selection course at Lackland Air Force Base in Texas.

<<< A Combat Controller candidate works out with a kettlebell.

Physical Tests

All candidates must pass the Physical Abilities and Stamina Test (PAST):

- Two x 65-foot (20-m) swims under water with three minutes rest between each (followed by a ten minute rest)
- 545-yard (500-m) swim in under fourteen minutes (followed by a thirty-minute rest)
- A 1.5-mile (2.4-km) run in 10 minutes 45 seconds (followed by a ten-minute rest)
- Minimum six pull-ups in under one minute (followed by a three-minute rest)

 Combat Control trainees do push-ups on the beach during a physical training session.

- Minimum 45 push-ups in under two minutes (followed by a three-minute rest)
- Minimum forty-five flutter kicks in under two minutes.

EYEWITNESS

"The reminders are constant. They're painted on the walls of the exclusive gym, screamed by instructors during intense physical training. Never quit."

—Army Times

COMBAT CONTROL OPERATOR COURSE

Being fit and determined is not enough. Combat Controllers also need good technical skills. This course covers navigation, communication and radar procedures, air traffic rules, and aircraft recognition.

A candidate attempts the "commando crawl" on the obstacle course during training.

A typical day on the Combat Control Operator Course starts at 6.30 a.m. with a 5-mile (8-km) run. During the day,

candidates might work out in the pool. Combat Controllers need to be just as at home in water as in the air and on land.

Obstacle Course

Friday is an extra tough day, with a 5-mile (8-km) rucksack march and an obstacle course. This is because, once special operations soldiers get to the battle zone, they need to be fit enough to fight.

The toughest part of the obstacle course is the commando crawl. This is an 83-foot (25-m) rope strung across a gap. Candidates must crawl along it upside down, relying on their arm strength to keep them from falling.

EYEWITNESS

"[Training] was definitely the hardest thing I've ever done, but the end result makes it all worth it. Combat Controller has without a doubt some of the toughest training the military has to offer. They're looking for quality over quantity."

—Michael Guzman, Airman 1st Class

A candidate raises his rucksack above his head during a "ruck press" as part of an extreme workout.

SPECIAL TACTICS ADVANCED SKILLS I

It takes a year to produce combat-ready Air Force special forces soldiers. Training is broken into four main phases, each focusing on a set of skills.

 Trainees listen to an instructor during an exercise in the swimming pool.

The first two phases of training prepare candidates for a range of operations in water and on land.

Phase 1: Water This is designed to turn candidates into combat divers who can

 Combat Controllers begin an exercise after being dropped off by helicopter.

infiltrate enemy areas underwater. Candidates must pass a range of tests, which include knot tying underwater, treading water with equipment, and buddy breathing, an emergency technique in which candidates share the same respirator underwater.

Phase 2: Ground This part of the course focuses on field training. Candidates learn about command and control missions and controlling the movement of aircraft. They practice calling for close fire support from airplanes and helicopters. Candidates

learn surveying and positioning techniques, and carry out Drop Zone and Landing Zone assault training missions and demolitions. They also have advanced communications training on different types of radio.

EYEWITNESS

"Combat Controllers are among the most highly trained personnel in the U.S. military. They maintain air traffic control qualification skills throughout their career in addition to other special operations skills."

—Air Force Special Operations Command

SPECIAL TACTICS ADVANCED SKILLS II

The second half of the Special Tactics Advanced Skills course focuses on making Combat Controllers effective members of other special forces teams in combat situations.

Combat Controller trainees deploy in a desert area during an exercise in Phase 3 of the Special Tactics Advanced Skills course.

There are two phases to this part of the course.

Phase 3: Employment
This phase teaches Combat

Controllers how to get in and out of operational areas. Training includes parachuting and fast-roping, underwater navigation, and insertions by boat or vehicle, as well as on foot.

Phase 4: Mission Qualification Training

This phase covers the strategic skills candidates need to plan a mission. They use these skills in a three-day exercise. They jump from a helicopter into the sea then go ashore to carry out covert reconnaissance of a target.

 Combat Controllers provide ground support as a C-130 Hercules takes off from an airstrip in Honduras during an exercise in the 1980s.

EYEWITNESS

"There are a lot of strong guys who can't do our job because they don't have the mental capacity, in particular the curiosity, to learn it. And there are a lot of smart guys who don't have the physical capacity or the physical drive to do it."

—Combat Controller, Iraq

►► SPECIALIST PARACHUTING

Free-fall parachute jumps are one of the best ways for Combat Controllers to enter enemy territory. High Altitude Low Opening (HALO) and High Altitude High Opening (HAHO) jumps allow aircraft to drop jumpers without being spotted by enemy radar.

When Combat Controllers jump as part of a team, they assemble in the air before opening their Ram-Air Parachute System (RAPS). In a HAHO jump, the jumpers glide toward a target up to 40 miles (65 km) away. They wear oxygen masks because of the altitude and carry altimeters to check when to open their parachutes. At night, the jumpers wear night-vision goggles to help them identify the drop zone.

◄◄ **A Combat Controller lands after a HALO jump. Jumpers only deploy their parachutes at heights below 6,000 feet (1,829 m).**

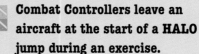
Combat Controllers leave an aircraft at the start of a HALO jump during an exercise.

Secret Arrival

At all times during and after the jump, a special forces team has to remain hidden. They land silently and quickly remove their parachutes. If necessary, they bury them nearby. Nothing is left in the drop zone that might give their presence away to the enemy.

If the jump has gone according to plan, the team will be close together. Once the last man has landed, they can regroup before moving ahead with the mission.

EYEWITNESS

"I can get to work in any manner— jumping, diving, walking, vehicle, boat, or submarine... When we get to work, our job is to talk on the radio and make things happen..."

—Paul Venturella, USAF Chief Master Sergeant

COMBAT DIVING

Combat diving training is tough. As part of the Combat Diving Qualification Course (CDQC), candidates have to be "drown proofed."

A two-man Combat Control team emerges from the water wearing wetsuits and SCUBA gear.

One of the main aims of combat diving training is to tackle the sense of panic most people feel if they are trapped underwater. Candidates undergo a series of tests in the safe environment of the pool. They have to swim 50 yards (45-m) underwater on one breath, for example.

《《 Waterproof kit enables Combat Controllers to go to work as soon as they leave the water.

Drown Proofing

For "drown proofing," the candidate's hands and feet are bound together with Velcro straps. They then have to bob up and down in 10 feet (3 m) of water for five minutes. They must not break the straps or touch the sides of the pool.

As part of drown proofing, swimmers have to pick up a face mask from the floor of the pool with their teeth. They must then do more bobs, while still holding the mask in their teeth.

EYEWITNESS

"The main reason combat diver qualification is so tough is when you take a human being, a common air-breather, put him under the water and take away his sources of air, it can make the biggest, meanest, baddest human being become very weak, panic-stricken. It drains the will to survive. We're looking for people who can overcome those pitfalls and remain confident."

—CDQC instructor

SUBMARINE OPERATIONS

Air Force Combat Controllers operate closely with U.S. Navy SEALs (Sea, Air, Land Teams). That means they need to be expert at the same kinds of water infiltration skills the SEALs use.

Water infiltration skills use submarines to get men into position without them being spotted by the enemy. Combat Controllers practice "lockouts," which is when they leave the submarine underwater by means of an airlock, as well as other forms of submarine insertion. On a covert offshore mission, for example, a submarine sometimes surfaces to allow combat rubber raiding craft

A Navy SEAL emerges from a Dry Deck Shelter on an underwater submarine.

 Combat Controllers prepare to launch a raiding craft from the deck of a submarine during an exercise.

(CRRC) to be launched from the deck. The Combat Controllers paddle ashore or use SCUBA gear to swim the last yards without creating the tell-tale bubbles.

Using a Dry Deck

If a submarine needs to stay submerged to avoid being seen, the raiding craft and other equipment for the mission are loaded in a Dry Deck Shelter. This is like a pod on the deck of the submarine. When it is opened,

EYEWITNESS

"The submarine provided that stealthy infiltration platform to get us as close to the objective as possible."

—USAF Colonel

the equipment is pushed out underwater. The CRRC is partly inflated and floats to the surface attached to a buoy line. The Combat Controller and Navy SEALs then complete the inflation of the boats and assemble the equipment on the surface.

⏵⏵ SCOUT SWIMMING

Scout swimming is a special kind of swimming in which special forces are trained to come ashore in pairs ready to fight.

An Air Force pararescueman practices swiftwater rescue in a river in Arizona.

Combat controllers practice scout swimming in the pool first. They need to be able to swim with uniforms and equipment. Then they start training in the sea. They learn how to handle a combat rubber raiding craft, including techniques for righting it if it flips over in the surf.

Washing Up

Combat Controllers learn "washing up," a technique for approaching the shore without being seen or heard. This is important when the enemy is close to the waterline. The scouts allow themselves to be carried forward by the movement of the water so that their own movements are minimized. The washing up routine is practiced after a jump from a helicopter into the sea. Once they reach the shore, scouts move quietly up the beach toward their objective.

Scout swimmers come ashore during a small-boat raid.

EYEWITNESS

"The term 'scout swimmers' refers to a pair of surface swimmers assigned a reconnaissance or security mission in advance of the boat or other swimmers. Scout swimmers secure the beach-landing site and evaluate it to ensure that it can accommodate the entire team."

—U.S. Army Field Manual

▶▶ SURVIVAL SKILLS (SERE)

Aircrew and special forces are both at higher risk of capture than other soldiers, because they often operate in or above enemy territory.

Combat Controllers are both airmen and special forces, so it is essential they learn survival, evasion, resistance, and escape techniques (SERE). They are taught to survive in extreme climates that have different challenges, from bitter cold in the Arctic to finding water and shelter from the sun in the heat of the desert. Combat Controllers learn to survive with their basic "escape kit." This contains survival essentials such as fishing lines, wire snares for catching small animals, and matches or flints for lighting fires.

◀◀ **A USAF survival expert demonstrates woodland camouflage during combat survival training.**

Survival Skills

Soldiers learn how to build shelters. These include snow caves for the Arctic and underground shelters in the desert. Combat Controllers learn how to lash together frames for shelters or logs for rafts. They also learn how to signal to aircraft and how to deal with medical problems. They learn about the psychological aspects of survival, so they can keep up their morale.

The escape and evasion parts of the course include learning to escape tracker dogs. The candidates also learn how to resist interrogation, and how to use the earliest opportunity to escape.

 Combat Controllers look on as SERE experts demonstrate a technique for entering a second-floor window.

IN ACTION

The survival skills Combat Controllers learn include wilderness living, shelter construction, fire building, map and compass navigation, backpacking, food and water procurement, wilderness medicine and first aid, and signaling.

MOUNTAIN OPERATIONS

Mountains can be useful locations. They give Combat Controllers good viewpoints over enemy positions and at the same time provide good concealment.

Combat Controllers and other members of Special Tactics Squadrons (STS) learn all about techniques to survive and fight in mountains. They learn about mountain walking and traversing techniques, and how to cross glaciers, which are huge ice sheets. They learn mountain-climbing techniques, such as finding hand holds and tying knots. They also learn rappelling and abseiling, in which they slide down rock faces on ropes. They learn how to belay, or fix ropes to a rock face for safer climbing.

An Air Force STS officer climbs on Mount Ranier, Washington, during the rescue of an injured airman.

 A Combat Controller climbs a rock face near Tucson, Arizona, during a training exercise.

Mountain Dangers

Mountains can be a dangerous environment, so Combat Controllers are taught to avoid risks if possible. They learn what to do if someone falls into a crevasse, or deep hole. If they fall into a crevasse themselves, they learn how to get out with a self-rescue technique that uses ropes and slip-knots.

One ever-present danger in the mountains is avalanches, so Combat Controllers learn avalanche awareness and survival. They watch out for signs of a possible avalanche, such as cracks in the snow. If they are caught in an avalanche, they learn to "swim" to the edge of the moving snow.

EYEWITNESS

"Mountain warfare is specialized combat with unique characteristics. Military leaders and soldiers need training and experience to understand the peculiarities of mountainous environments and how they affect combat. Armies that train for mountain combat perform much better than those that do not."

—**Military Review**

NAVIGATION AND COMMUNICATIONS

A Combat Controller cannot do his job if he cannot communicate instructions to aircraft. To give accurate orders, he must know precisely where he is.

The key part of the Combat Controllers' role is to communicate information from the ground to the air. If they are setting up an assault zone or calling in air attacks, they have to be able to report highly accurate geographical coordinates. They are all highly skilled navigators, who

Combat Controllers use a map to pinpoint landing zone locations.

 A Combat Controller communicates with a Navy F/A-18 Super Hornet as part of Operation Spartan Shield, an exercise held in West Asia in 2012.

can use maps or the most up-to-date global positioning system (GPS) devices to find their precise location. They also use electronic devices to gather sophisticated information about enemy positions.

Reporting Back

To communicate information to aircraft, Combat Controllers rely on their radios, which can transmit in short bursts, to help prevent the signal being intercepted by the enemy. Controllers also have to be able to improvise if something goes wrong. For that reason they are all experts at using a range of satellite technology to establish radio connections.

IN ACTION

Radio signals are vital to Combat Controllers, but they can be intercepted and betray a Combat Controller's location. Short-burst radios compress messages so they take less time to send. That cuts the chances of a signal being intercepted.

▶▶ SETTING UP ASSAULT ZONES

Combat Controllers were created to set up assault zones. They infiltrate hostile territory and must identify an area where a main force can be dropped safely by parachute or landed by helicopter.

An Army colonel packs up his parachute after landing in a zone identified by USAF Combat Controllers.

The Combat Controllers move quickly to establish the assault zone. They remove any obstacles, such as unexploded bombs or

Combat Controllers use night-vision goggles to scan an area while on deployment in Afghanistan in May 2012.

mines, from the area, carrying out controlled demolition. They set up markers for pilots and parachutists. Once the zone is secured, they establish air traffic control (ATC) clearance and provide instructions for any aircraft entering the area.

Source of Information

Once the assault zone is ready, the Combat Control team relays as much information as possible to the mission commanders. This might include reports from intelligence personnel, details of the local weather situation, and details of possible routes for casualty extraction.

EYEWITNESS

"*I can put a guy on a motorcycle, and he can pull portable lights out of his rucksack, shortly after landing at the location, to mark a runway.*"

—Colonel Michael Sneeder, commander, 22nd STS

▶▶ AIRCRAFT

Air Force Combat Controllers are linked with aircraft of all types. They use airplanes and helicopters to get into and out of war zones. They can also call upon a range of air support for ground missions.

One of the most useful tools is the Puma Unmanned Aerial Vehicle (UAV). This small unmanned aircraft system, or drone, helps Combat Controllers gather intelligence, surveillance, reconnaissance, and targeting data (ISRT). The UAV is fitted with optical and infrared cameras that gather information about the enemy. The UAV can fly for

Combat Controllers launch a Puma UAV from a rooftop in an urban combat environment.

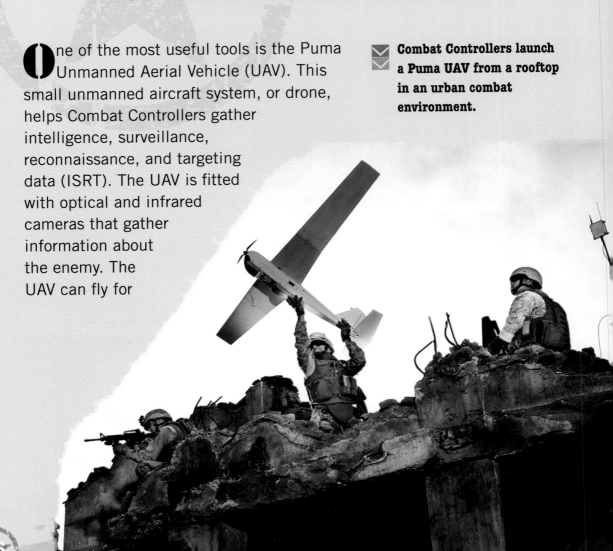

 The AC-130H/U Spectre gunship has weapons ranged along either side of its fuselage.

over three hours. It is controlled remotely through a handset or via GPS-based navigation.

Spectre AC-130U

Combat Controllers call in this gunship, known as the "Spooky," to provide close air support for missions. It supports ground troops, escorts convoys, and provides support for urban operations. Pilots use a flying technique known as the pylon turn. This is when the aircraft banks toward the target, allowing the gunners to keep firing at the target at all times.

EYEWITNESS

"When you're pinned down and can't move, having eyes in the sky to take out the enemy is pretty instrumental in making sure your guys come back alive."

—Major Charlie Hodges, Combat Controller

WHEELED VEHICLES

As with other special forces, Combat Controllers rely on lightweight vehicles to move quickly to key positions.

Combat Controllers' motorbikes are so tough they can be simply thrown out of an airplane or helicopter.

One of the favored vehicles is the motorcycle. The Kawasaki KLR250-D8 motorbike is used by a variety of special operations forces. It has infrared headlights, so the driver can see at night without showing a visible light, and it has

 A soldier uses an LTATV during an exercise in joint forcible entry, when special forces fight their way into enemy territory.

a bracket for carrying a personal weapon. The bike is painted with camouflage paint with a low infrared signature. Mufflers are fitted to the exhaust. The bike can be dropped by parachute on a special palette to prevent damage.

Lightweight Tactical All-Terrain Vehicle (LTATV)

This is a lightweight vehicle that carries two Combat Controllers. It has no armor, but makes up for that lack of protection by being very fast.

It can carry more equipment than a motorcycle but it is still highly mobile in areas that might not be accessible by larger vehicles. The LTATV can be carried in MH-47 Chinook and CV-22 Osprey aircraft, or it can be dropped by parachute.

IN ACTION

The Kawasaki KLX110 is a mini motorbike. It is strong but small enough to be dropped by parachute or fixed to the side of a helicopter or a land vehicle. Combat Controllers use it to carry out reconnaissance for drop zones and airfields.

▶▶ RIFLES AND HANDGUNS

Although the job of a Combat Controller is to get other soldiers into position ready to fight, operating deep inside enemy territory means they have to be ready to defend themselves.

Combat Controllers are trained to use a wide range of weapons, including those used by other special forces.

MK17 SCAR-H

The Special Operations Forces Combat Assault Rifle (SCAR) was developed especially for U.S. special forces. The heavy version of the rifle, the SCAR-H, fires 7.62mm bullets. It comes with either a long or a short barrel. The rifle has a rail system for accessories, such as sights.

M4 Carbine

The M4 is a magazine-fed light rifle that is capable of providing rapid

◀◀ **The SCAR-H is available in a long or short-barreled version, as seen here.**

 This SCAR-H has been fitted with advanced sights and with a laser beam that points at the target.

fire at close range. The M4 can also be adapted to carry a range of accessories on a rail system, including a close-combat optic sight.

M9 Pistol

This pistol has a fifteen-round magazine and is designed to work in even the most extreme conditions, including after immersion in salt water or burial in sand, mud, or snow. It can also withstand temperatures as low as -40° or as high as 140°F (-40° to 60°C).

MK-17 SCAR-H
Ammunition: 7.62mm
Range: 600m standard
Length: 965mm (stock extended/ standard)

M4 CARBINE
Ammunition: 5.56mm
Range: 500m
Weight: 2.88kg
Length: 840mm (standard)

M9 SEMI-AUTOMATIC PISTOL
Caliber: 9x19mm Parabellum
Weight: 952g unloaded
Length: 217mm
Effective range: 50m

>> FIGHTING THE TALIBAN

On February 6, 2011, a Combat Controller was attached to a group of Army Green Beret Special Forces for a mission to capture territory from the Taliban in Helmand Province, Afghanistan.

A Combat Controller on horseback with local Afghan fighters during the advance on the Taliban.

As they entered the area, the U.S. soldiers were attacked by enemy insurgents with small-arms and mortar fire and improvised explosive devices. The special forces continued to advance and

took control of an area where they then dug in. Although they faced overwhelming odds, the special forces had a secret weapon: the Combat Controller. Under fire, he called in unmanned aerial vehicles (UAV) to bomb the enemy.

The mission had been planned to last a week. In fact, it lasted eighteen days, during which the Combat Controller coordinated the attacks of up to forty aircraft, dropping over 30,000 tons of bombs.

 A Combat Controller takes cover with a special forces team.

IN ACTION

Combat Controllers can direct very precise air support. In Helmand, the Combat Controller helped rescue a wounded special forces solider. He called in close air support to clear insurgents and allow the patrol to fight its way back to the U.S. position.

>> OPERATIONS IN IRAQ

The United States led an invasion of Iraq in 2003. In early 2007, U.S. forces and their Iraqi allies were still fighting insurgents who were rebelling against the U.S.-backed government.

When Iraqi police in the town of Najaf tried to arrest insurgents from a group called the "Soldiers of Heaven," they were ambushed by about 800 fighters. Two U.S. Army Special Forces units were sent to the rescue, each with its own USAF Combat

>> Combat Controllers watch as an F-15 airstrike they have called fires on an enemy position.

Controller. The Combat Controllers called in close air support to bomb and strafe the enemy positions.

 A Combat Controller calls in an airstrike on a house occupied by insurgents in Iraq in 2008.

Close Air Support

A third Special Forces unit arrived. It was pinned down by 40 insurgents in a strongpoint. Despite being dangerously close to the target, the USAF Combat Controller called in a laser-guided bomb. A direct hit killed many insurgents. The Combat Controller and two Green Berets stormed the position and killed the rest. The destruction of the strongpoint turned the battle in the favor of the U.S. and their allies.

IN ACTION

Combat Controllers take educated risks. The "safe" range for a 500-pound (226-kg) bomb is about 985 feet (300 m). In Najaf, the U.S. unit was only 330 feet (100 m) from the enemy bunker. The strike was called because of the danger of the situation.

GLOSSARY

abseil To descend a rock face by sliding down ropes.

air traffic control Controlling the safe movement of aircraft.

belay To fix ropes to pins for rock climbing.

camouflage To use colors to make something blend with the surroundings.

close-air support Using gunfire and missiles from aircraft to help soldiers on the ground.

crevasse A deep crack in a glacier.

deploy To move troops into position to fight.

glacier A thick, slow-moving sheet of ice.

GPS Global Positioning System, a location system that uses satellite technology.

infiltrate To move into position without being spotted by the enemy.

lockout Leaving a submarine underwater by using an air lock.

meteorologist Someone who studies and forecasts the weather.

navigation The act of finding out one's geographical location and planning a route.

operational area The location where a mission takes place.

pararescueman A medical expert trained in prachuting and the rescue of casualties from war zones.

pathfinder A soldier who goes ahead of a main force and marks their route.

rappel To slide quickly down a rope.

reconnaissance Observation of an enemy's positions.

SCUBA An abbreviation for Self-Contained Underwater Breathing Apparatus, a device for breathing underwater.

stealth Techniques for moving without being noticed.

surveillance Close observation of the enemy.

FURTHER INFORMATION

BOOKS

Masters, Nancy Robinson. *Pararescue Jumper.* Cool Military Careers. North Mankato, MN: Cherry Lake Publishing, 2012.

Porterfield, Jason. *USAF Special Tactics Teams.* Inside Special Operations. New York, NY: Rosen Central, 2008.

Roberts, Jeremy. *U.S. Air Force Special Operations.* U.S. Armed Forces. Minneapolis, MN: Lerner Publishing Group, 2004.

Rose, Simon. *Air Force Special Operations.* US Armed Forces. New York, NY: AV2 by Wiegl, 2013.

Ryan, Peter. *Black Ops and Other Special Missions of the U.S. Air Force Combat Control Team.* Inside Special Forces. New York, NY: Rosen Central, 2012.

Vanderhoof, Gabrielle. *Air Force.* Special Forces: Protecting, Building, Teaching, and Fighting. Broomall, PA: Mason Crest Publishers, 2010.

WEBSITES

ccshf.org
Website of the Combat Control School and Heritage Foundation, with features about combat control in the past and present.

www.afsoc.af.mil/library/ afsocheritage/
Air Force Special Operations Command pages on their history.

www.menshealth.com/best-life/ special-military-operators
Article on Combat Controllers from *Men's Health* magazine.

www.military.com/special-operations/ air-force-combat-controllers.html
Military.com site about training to become a Combat Controller.

Publisher's note to educators and parents: Our editors have carefully reviewed these websites to ensure that they are suitable for students. Many websites change frequently, however, and we cannot guarantee that a site's future contents will continue to meet our high standards of quality and educational value. Be advised that students should be closely supervised whenever they access the Internet.

INDEX